Options Trading
Secret Strategies That Made Me $30,597 In 23 Days

[DAN KING]

Legal & Disclaimer

The information contained in this book and its contents is not designed to replace or take the place of any form of medical or professional advice; and is not meant to replace the need for independent medical, financial, legal or other professional advice or services, as may be required. The content and information in this book has been provided for educational and entertainment purposes only.

The content and information contained in this book has been compiled from sources deemed reliable, and it is accurate to the best of the Author's knowledge, information and belief. However, the Author cannot guarantee its accuracy and validity and cannot be held liable for any errors and/or omissions. Further, changes are periodically made to this book as and when needed. Where appropriate and/or necessary, you must consult a professional (including but not limited to your doctor, attorney, financial advisor or such other professional advisor) before using any of the suggested remedies, techniques, or information in this book.

Upon using the contents and information contained in this book, you agree to hold harmless the Author from and against any damages, costs, and expenses, including any legal fees potentially resulting from the application of any of the information provided by this book. This disclaimer applies to any loss, damages or injury caused by the use and application, whether directly or indirectly, of any advice or information presented, whether for breach of contract, tort, negligence, personal injury, criminal intent, or under any other cause of action.

You agree to accept all risks of using the information presented inside this book.

You agree that by continuing to read this book, where appropriate and/or necessary, you shall consult a professional (including but not limited to your doctor, attorney, or financial advisor or such other advisor as needed) before using any of the suggested remedies, techniques, or information in this book.

Table of Contents

Introductions

An option is defined as a contract between two parties, which gives the holder (buyer) the right, but not the obligation, to buy or sell the underlying asset at an agreed fixed price at an agreed time in the future – or in some cases at any time before the contract's expiry date.

Options as we saw earlier were designed to allow institutional investors to mitigate risk and act as tools for ensuring against market unpredictability. Thus the Options contract was originally used to buy insurance against potentially catastrophic price movements that would have led to huge losses. But their inherent characteristics soon made Options attractive to traders as speculation tools in their own right. To see how Option became fashionable with traders we need to take a deeper dive into what makes up an Option contract.

An option is a contract based upon an underlying asset, a derivative, which means that an Option's value is derived from the underlying asset. In financial trading the underlying asset is usually stocks or a commodity, but it also can be the value of a market index or interest rate. Indeed in contract law it can be practically anything.

Options in Common Law

Options can be best explained and easiest understood using examples from everyday contract law as Option contracts have been in place since trade began. For example, suppose you want to buy a house or a new car, but you don't have a mortgage or finance at hand. In this case you would perhaps agree with a price with the seller and a date for completion of the sale. However the seller is going to want a deposit in return for this sales contingency, which gives you the right to buy at the agreed price at a future date or walk away from the sale if you change your mind. The deposit is compensation to the seller for providing you with the right, but not the obligation, to buy the car or house at the agreed price and date. If you renege on the deal and walk away, you will lose the deposit as that is the price of that option.

This is the basis of financial options, and if we consider the transaction through the lens of a financial trade we can substitute many of the technical terms to make the metaphor more transparent. So for example when you go to buy a house you agree to a price (strike price) and a date (expiry date) and a suitable deposit (premium) as part of the sales contingency (the Option contract). Then on the expiry date you will exercise your right to buy the house (stock) at the strike price or walk away (let the option expire) losing your deposit (premium).

Don't worry too much about some of the terms, such as strike price and premium all the trading jargon will be explained soon enough. What is important just now is that you understand that with Options trading you are dealing with a contract, the right to buy rather than the asset itself. But because that contract has inherent value, as it derives its value from the relationship between the strike prices, which is fixed in the contract, relative to the current market stock price. And if the contract is deemed attractive to others in the market then it also becomes a tradable asset in its own right.

Types of options

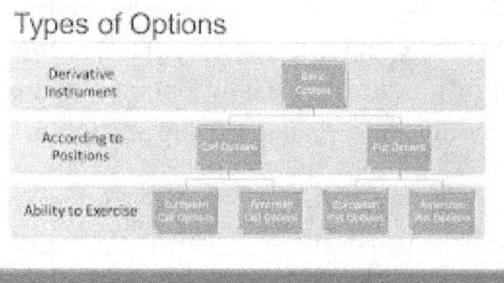

When it comes to options, there are going to be two different types of options that you can work with. There will be the call options. These will give the buyer the right to purchase the underlying security of the contract at a fixed price. This would be like the example that we talked about above. There is also the put options, which includes options that give the buyer the right to sell the underlying security at a fixed price.

The biggest thing to remember here is that when working with the call option, the buyer of this option can only start to profit from that option if the value of the underlying stock or underlying index goes up. But in the other case with the put option, the buyer of the option can only start to profit when the value of the underlying stock or index goes down.

The benefits and the negatives of working with options

We have spent a bit of time taking a look at options and what they are all about. There will also be a ton of strategies that you are able to use when you decide to get into this kind of market and we will talk about them more as we go. But at this point, you may be wondering why a trader would be willing to start in the options market at all. It often seems more complicated than other forms of investing, and a new options trading investor may wonder if the risk is worth the profits in the long run?

There are a number of reasons why people would choose to work in the options market as their investment choice. First, an investor is able to profit on changes that occur in an assets price on the market, without ever having to put money up to purchase that equity. They do have to pay a premium on that, but they don't have to pay the full price of the asset in order to enter the market. The premium that needs to be paid is going to come in at a fraction of the cost of what the investor would pay if they bought that asset outright. This can help them to leverage their account more to get into a bigger trade, without having a lot of capital to start with.

Another benefit is that when an investor buys an options instead of just purchasing an equity, they are able to earn more per dollar that they invested compared to what they can do on the traditional stock market. This means that you have more potential profits than you would with traditional investing. But keep in mind that this also means there is more potential for losses with this trading as well.

Except when selling uncovered puts or calls, the risk that comes with options trading is going to be limited. When you purchase the option, the risk that you take on is going to be limited to the amount of premium that you were paying for the option, no matter how much the price of the stock moves against the strike price that you set.

With all of these benefits, it is a wonder why everyone doesn't decide to join the options trading market and use this as their investment tool to make a lot of money. But, just like with all the other investment types that you may try, options do have some main characteristics that will make a few investors turn away and look for other opportunities.

First, when you first enter into the market, you will find that these options are going to be time sensitive. A contract for an option is going to be for a short period of time, usually no more than a few months. It is also possible that as the buyer, you could lose all of your investment, even if you make a good prediction about which way the price moves and the magnitude of the price change. If the price change doesn't occur before the expiry date, you still lose out on your investment.

That time sensitivity can make it hard for a lot of people. It is a big risk to try and figure out the exact time frames for when certain actions are going to occur. If you are off by even one day, that means that you would lose out on the whole investment. But since these contracts can't be left for too long, and leaving them for longer than necessary can result in the stock reversing as well, this is a risk that many options traders have to deal with.

In addition, you will find that many investors consider options as a less tangible choice compared to the other investment types that you can choose. For example, if you purchase a stock, you will get a certificate that shows you own a part of the company. Even a Certificate of Deposit investment from the bank will do this for you. But as an investor in options, the purchase is going to be considered a book entry only investment. You don't technically own the asset that you are working with, you only own the contract and get the choice of exercising your right to purchase or sell that asset at a later time.

There are a lot of mixed reviews out there when it comes to options and how well they can be used for investment purposes. For some investors, these are the perfect vehicles to help them limit their risks a bit and increase the amount of profit that they are able to earn. For others, they are just too risky and they would rather find other, more safe, options that will help them to earn a good return on investment.

What is all comes down to is the fact that options and options trading just aren't the right fit for every investor. And just because you have heard of other people having success with options trading in the past doesn't mean that it is the right one for you. Options are going to be a risky type of investment, but they also provide you with a ton of opportunities to make a profit for investors who are willing to learn the ropes and who will use this financial instrument to help them make more money

Chapter 1: Options Trading Explained

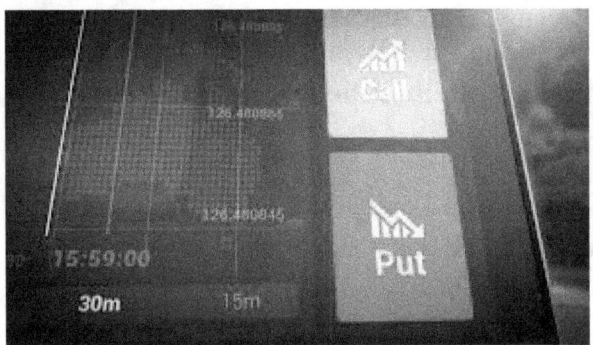

At their most basic, options are a type of security that can be traded, in much the same way as more traditional stocks and bonds. Essentially, when you purchase an option you are purchasing a contract that gives you the ability to either buy or sell a specific type of asset at a certain price for a certain period of time. While this may seem complicated, in reality, it is much the same process that anyone who has ever purchased a home via a loan has been through.

In this case, the buyer and the seller make an agreement for the price of the house and then the price of the house is confirmed, even if it takes a while for the process of obtaining a loan from the bank to be completed. In the interim the housing market could change in such a way that the price of the home has increased dramatically, which would be good for the buyer, or the price of the home could decrease significantly, at which time the buyer could withdraw their offer. Either way, the contract (or option) protects the buyer to ensure they get a specific deal regardless of what happens between the point the contract is agreed upon until its expiration date.

There are many different types of options, though this guide is going to focus largely on stock options, and they can all be broken down into two primary categories those that are calls or those that are puts.

Calls: When you are going to buy a specific option, this action is referred to as a call. When you call an option, you are doing so with the assumption that the underlying stock related to that option is going to increase in value before your call expires so you can sell the stock for a profit. If you exercise your company stock options, you are calling those options.

Puts: If you are selling a specific stock at a specific price you are instead creating a put option. In this instance you hope that the stock you are selling is going to decrease in price significantly before the option expires which is how you make money in this case. Puts are also often used by those who already own shares of a risky stock to protect their primary investment. Exotic options vary in many more ways and should not be considered until you are comfortable with everything vanilla options have to offer.

Furthermore, there are additional broad categories that all options, be they puts or calls, also fall into. The following are what are known as **vanilla options** which are those with specifications you are going to run into most often.

American options: Regardless of where it originates, an option is considered an American option if it can be acted upon at any point prior to its expiration time.

European options: Regardless of where it originates, an option is considered to be a European option if it can only be acted upon at the precise moment it expires.

Short options: An option with an expiration date of minutes, hours or days is said to be a short option

Long options: Long options are those that do not expire for a year or more which makes them better suited for long term investing instead of daily trading. Long options are sometimes referred to as long equity anticipation securities or LEAPS.

Additionally, those who actively trade options can be grouped into 4 categories, **holders** are those who buy options and those who sell them are referred to as **writers**. From there, holders and writers are broken down based on whether they work mostly in calls or mostly in puts. Of the pair, holders have more power than writers because they have a choice to either use an option to buy the related stock in question or to let the time run out on the option if the market didn't move in the way they expected. Writers, on the other hand, are limited in what they can do based on what the holder in question decides upon.

Options Lingo

While there is little going on in an options exchange that is all that opaque, the amount of obscure sounding jargon that the average options trader can spew in under 30 seconds can make the process more intimidating than it ultimately needs to be. Do yourself a favor and become familiar with the following words and phrases and you'll be well on your way to sounding like a professional or at least not becoming lost in their conversations.

Strike price: The strike price is the starting price of the stock you are buying the option to purchase or sell depending if you are creating a call or a put.

Exercise: If the market moves in such a way that the amount of your strike price sounds appealing and you want to sell or buy the stock at the price in question then you are said to be exercising the option.

Trading out: If you as the holder agree to sell an option, the writer of that same option can then purchase it back in a process known as trading out. This is how more than 50 percent of all options trades end. Only 10 percent of options are ever fully exercised.

Listed: If an option is listed on a national exchange it is said to be listed. Listed options have clear strike prices as well as clear expiration dates which makes them a great place for new options traders to start. Listed options are most likely going to deal in 100 shares of stock of the related stock.

Underlying stock: The underlying stock of an option is the specific stock that the option is dealing in.

In the money: On a call, if the price of the underlying stock rises above the stock price then that option is said to be in the money.

Intrinsic value: When a call is in the money, the difference between the current price and the strike price is referred to as its intrinsic value.

Time value: How much time a specific option has until it expires is said to be its time vale.

Volatility: If the underlying stock related to a particular option is prone to extreme fluctuations in price with little warning then it is said to have a high level of volatility.

Premium: The total price of the option in question including a combination of stock price, strike price, time value and volatility.

Primary uses for options investing

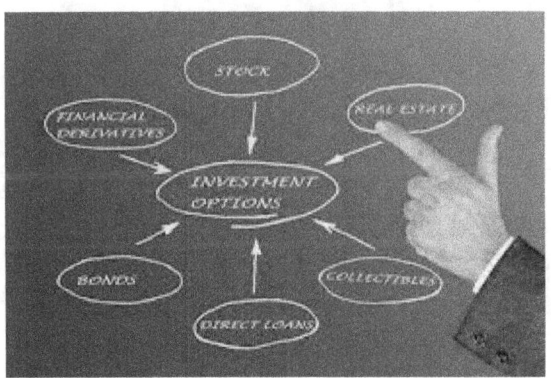

Professional options investors utilize options in two main ways, to minimize the risk of other investments or to bet on the way the market is going to be heading in the near future. Betting on the market is referred to as speculation and options traders who can read the market can use it to make money regardless of the direction the market is heading in. Speculators need to know how the market is going to move but also the speed at which it is going to do so which is why speculation can be responsible for huge financial swings in both directions. The volatility comes from the fact that each option is 100 shares so relatively small movements in the underlying stock can lead to significant movement in related options.

While speculation can be risky, using options to hedge other investments is anything but. In this scenario, the options the trader purchases are essentially a type of insurance that protects other investments the trader has made. This is particularly helpful if another investment is a stock that has a high volatility as a put option will allow the trader to ensure they at least get their money back if the stock price of the underlying stock drops dramatically. Likewise, if the underlying stock dramatically increases in value then the trader can let the option expire and only be out the related fees paid on the options trade. This process means that traders can pursue risky but potentially profitable trades while protecting themselves as much as possible.

Know what to expect

If you are planning to trade successfully on a regular basis, the first thing you are going to need to work on is removing your emotions from the process completely. Your goal will be to create a trading plan (discussed in chapter 4) which you can stick to completely, which will make it easier for you to make the right choices even if several trades have not gone in your favor and your emotions are getting the better of you.

The first step in this process, however, is to have a realistic idea of just what to expect from your initial foray into options trading. This means getting rid of any flights of fancy that you might have that tell you that you will get rich after just a few trades and that you don't need to do any research and can instead rely on your gut to see the types of long term results you are looking for. Additionally, you will want to start by keeping a journal of the emotions you feel through each part of the trade in question so that you can look back on them later on and get a clear idea of when you are likely to experience what type of emotion and why.

As a general rule, the biggest cause for concern among new options traders stems from the fact that they expect things to always go according to plan. In fact, this is never going to be the case 100 percent of the time and even a tried and true system is never going to turn out perfect results, that's why investing in options is considered riskier than some other types of investing you might choose. You will find this fact easier to accept if, instead of focusing on whether or not each trade made money, you focus on following your system to the letter every time and not letting emotion or the results of the previous trades distract you from following through in the best way possible.

Successful options traders are those who follow their systems to the letter and let the fact that their system average is above 50 percent guarantee that they are going to make money in the long term. With this in mind, you will find it easier to deal with losing trades in the moment and also find it easier to choose reliable options trades over those that offer high margins for both risk and reward. This mindset will be easier to think about achieving than actually achieving and first, but it is important to keep in mind the fact that the longer you practice restraint, the easier it will be to practice it in the future.

Chapter 2: Managing Option Positions

Rolling positions

What is rolling?

Sometimes options traders wish to make adjustments to positions they hold in the market. When this happens, it means the trader's market outlook has changed. It is actually possible to roll a short or long option position.

The term rolling refers to changing the outlook on the underlying security of an option. This change is often driven by a change in the outlook of the markets and positions held on certain trades. In such situations, a trader is often worried that certain positions will be assigned.

Rolling is similar to making a different turn other than the one initially planned. Think, for instance, you leave home heading to the grocery store only to end up at the movies. This is very similar to what rolling is about.

The aim of rolling is to either deter or cancel the assignment. Basically, managing positions through rolling is an advanced technique that should only be applied by seasoned traders and experienced investors. Therefore, as an intermediate trader, you need to ensure that you thoroughly understand this process before applying it.

Rolling a position

Anytime that a trader rolls a position, he or she will be purchasing options very close to a current position in the marketing then sell this position in order to start another one. This process will cause small, minute but significant tweaks to the strike prices of options held by the trader. The effect of this move will be to shift the expiration times further out, so positions do not expire as initially planned. Even then, this process is not a guarantee that the strategy will work. In extreme cases, rolling will only compound losses, so it is advisable that only experienced traders apply this technique.

How to Roll the Short Strangle

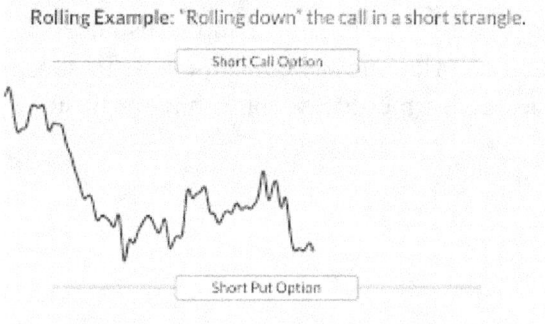

Rolling Example: 'Rolling down' the call in a short strangle.

Rolling is the process of making adjustments to options strategies that a trader sets up. There are varied reasons why traders actually make adjustments to their trades. These include erroneous initial predictions, changing market positions, and news that will affect the performance of a stock.

Now on a strangle strategy you always have a negative delta on the put and a positive delta on the call option. Therefore, we can deduce that we have a neutral delta in this instance. A neutral delta is okay at the onset. However, if the position remains that way then you lose money. As a trader, your desire is to make money; therefore, when there is movement in the stock price you want this movement to be huge. As such you may use gamma which will ensure the price goes up. However, should the stock price remain constant without any movement then you will lose money.

The short strangle is sometimes considered by traders as a very risky strategy. However, as an experienced trader who knows what he is doing; this is not necessarily the case. Here is a look at some circumstances where risk is reduced by rolling action.

First of all, premium is considered rather rich. As it is, a short straddle requires a trader to sell a put option, and a call option based on an underlying option with similar expiration dates and strike price. The best ones are the ones that offer a very rich premium under near-the-money or at-the-money conditions.

Also, it is crucial that short straddles have expiration dates that are within one month or less. It is time decay that causes the value of options to decline. This is why short straddles should be limited to only short-term options. Time decay often happens extremely fast within the first month.

Traders should focus their eyes on the current price, and the strike price then note the relationship. It is advisable to close positions once it becomes practically possible. This should happen especially when positions begin to move in the money. It is always a great idea to close at a profit because time decay will affect the value of the trade.

Also, keep a lookout for time decay. Therefore, once it begins to occur, you should plan to close the positions entered. Also, it is advisable to consider duplicating the strategy should the intrinsic value advance too fast. The forward movement in some instance can be unavoidable depending on certain factors such as price movement direction. In short, the price of the stock will not be volatile and as such time decay could have a positive effect on the two sides.

Adjusting a Butterfly to a Condor

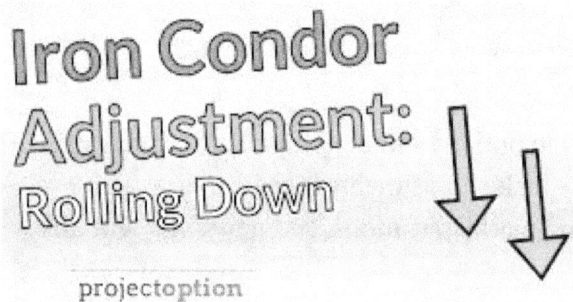

As a trader, you may set up a butterfly position which may then experience certain challenges that may cost you significant losses. One of the options you may want to consider is turning the position from a butterfly to a condor. A butterfly spread can easily be split into two distinct spreads.

Ideally, you will want to split the original butterfly and create an additional butterfly. When you do this, you will come up with a condor. You will still have two spreads but with completely different sold strikes. At this juncture, you would not necessarily adjust the butterfly. However, the intervention is necessary especially when the price of the underlying stock was rising and while other indicators showed the option was headed towards a loss.

Making such adjustments is necessary especially where losses seem inevitable based on conditions, but the situation can be rescued. But the interventions should be designed and implemented based on market trends, conditions, volatility, price action, and other related factors.

Rolling a Short Call Spread

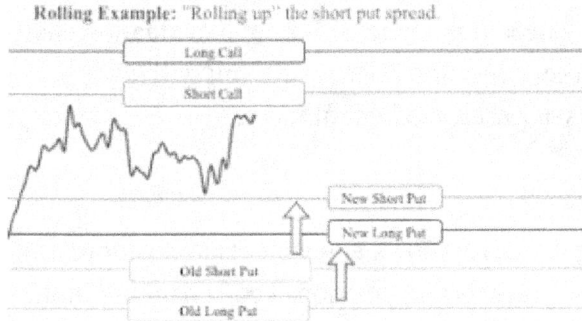

When you roll a spread, the action is similar to rolling a single option. A trader who rolls a short call spread is most probably exit a position in a timely fashion with the strike prices moving down or up. The difference between rolling the short call spread and an individual option is that with the short call spread you will be engaged in a four-way trade. You will essentially be trading four different options instead of the usual two. This means opening two new positions while closing two existing ones.

How to Roll a Covered Call

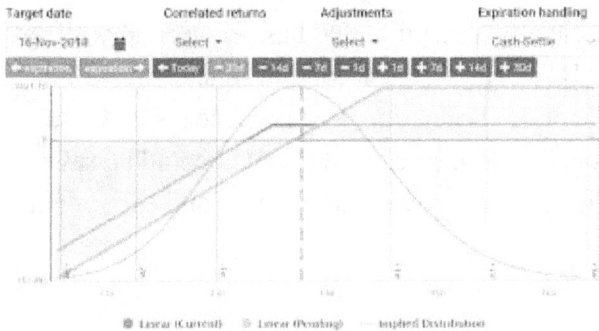

When you hold covered calls, you can choose to sell them in order to reduce the cost of holding them in long positions. When rolling calls forward, you will improve the break-even position and make it easier to be successful in the long run. However, you need to know if a position should be rolled on and when to do so. For instance, should rolling of a position occur 20 days to expiration or possibly at expiration?

Also, just about any trader can write a covered call. The most crucial thing is to manage such a position appropriately. Certain factors should be considered when rolling a position especially near expiration Fridays.

First, you need to confirm whether the underlying stock is suitable for this kind of management. Then you will need to confirm the option chains for statistics involving current and next month.

Now use the Ellman Calculator and enter the statistics in order to determine whether the dates are viable for rolling management. The 1-month goal for initial returns stands at 2% to 4%. With this information, you will finally need to conduct a thorough evaluation chart technical information and the prevailing market conditions. This way, you will comfortably be able to make adjustments to your trades to benefit more.

Rolling out a Butterfly Position

As a trader, you need to have a great trading plan that allows adjustments to positions that you have taken in the market. This is because markets and positions keep changing in the course of a trading period. Therefore it is advisable to work within a set of guidelines rather than a set of strict rules.

Rolling other Positions

You can also implement the rolling process as a management action on all other positions when the need arises. Sometimes you can roll up a position and other times you get to roll down on positions.

Rolling up a position

The term rolling up refers to the process of closing a position that has been set up while at the same time opening up another position. However, in the second instance, you will be using options that have a much higher strike price. When you do this, it means that you are essentially rolling up your position to a higher strike price. While you could be saving your positions from losses, rolling up also helps to improve your position and earn you a higher profit.

Rolling up long and short options

You can roll up all sorts of positions whether you are short on certain positions or long on others. Alternatively, you can close a position in order to save yourself from losses or a worse position. This process is similar when applied to call options as when it is applied to put options.

As you roll up your short option positions or even long positions, you will basically be switching your existing ones for others with contracts that are cheaper and hence affordable. Basically, cheapest contracts are those with highest strike prices. When rolling output options, the process will involve changing current options position to another position that has more costly contracts. This is because puts with a higher strike price are also generally more costly. However, the situation will also depend on whether you are holding a short or a long position.

Net cash gain

You can expect net cash benefit if you roll a long position. The reason is that you will get into a cheaper position after selling your previous position. When it comes to short call positions, you may be required to pay a higher price for contracts, and in return, you will get as the new contracts will be at a higher price.

Also, when you roll a long position on a put option, this basically means that you will sell contracts constituting your current position at a low price and then purchase costly positions. Therefore, when you roll up a short position on put options, you will basically be closing the same positions through purchasing of lower cost contracts followed by writing more costly contracts.

Why roll up positions?

Rolling up options positions is crucial in a number of ways especially to options traders. The most important aspect is to understand the exact reason why a position should be rolled up. One reason is that you may want to avoid assignment of share contracts that you own especially when you are in short option call positions.

In other instances, you may want to roll up positions of call options that you hold. This happens mostly when stock prices shoot upwards unexpectedly. This rise in stock price before the expiration of a contract before expiration may alter your position and predictions. To prevent your contracts from being assigned, you will need to roll your position and attain a higher strike which will be out of the money.

When you hold a long position on an option, you will want to roll the position so that you end up with a higher strike price especially if the underlying stock is deep in the money after the price rises steeply. This way, you will be able to profit from your current position even as you continue to predict and speculate on the future performance of the stocks and options that you hold but without putting your profits at risk.

Supposing you had positions on long put options and your predictions indicate that the value of the underlying stock will fall drastically. However, your predictions were inaccurate, and the stocks actually go up. In this instance, you do not want to suffer any losses so you may decide to roll your position. This will help you hedge your losses. The best instance, in this case, would be to sell your put options that are out of the money. This way, you stand a great chance of recouping some extrinsic value. And then you will buy additional put options whose strike price is higher than the previous one. You will, therefore, benefit more even if the stock price was to fail from this point.

Risks with rolling process

It is important to note that there are certain risks involved when applying this technique. This tends to happen when the market moves pretty fast in one direction or when volatility is significantly high. There could be a major impact on your positions when the options prices fluctuate in a major way.

Also, anytime that there is a time delay with two distinct but related orders with price changes involved, then there will be a challenge known as slippage. The term slippage refers to a challenge encountered by traders when they place different orders that converge towards a single position. There is a good solution to this problem that is available and regularly used by options traders.

Traders prefer to roll up in order to avoid or evade this specific challenge. This mostly involves closing out one order and then investing in another order that has much higher strike prices.

Benefits of rolling out an option

There are definite benefits of rolling out an options position. Most of the time rolling out helps to prevent traders from incurring losses due to inaccurate predictions or unexpected market movements. In other cases, traders use rolling techniques to adjust their positions for increased profitability. They tend to earn more money from their positions by rolling operations.

Also, it is a fact that most rollout processes are conducted through a single transaction rather than multiple ones. As such, they cost less and hence save a trader from incurring much higher prices compared to closing out a position then opening new ones. This also includes paying for contracts and commissions. This way, traders tend to save money even though this is not necessarily the reason why traders roll out positions.

If you conduct plenty of transactions, then such savings will come in handy. It is crucial at this stage to remember that rolling out on options positions generally depends on your outlook on positions more than anything else.

> Traders also get to avoid the situation where they lose out due to what is referred to as price slippage. This is a situation that occurs when in between different opening and closing transactions. As a trader, it is advisable to always be on the lookout for savings and profit generation. Smart traders take all opportunities to avoid costs, save money, and earn profits.

Chapter 3: Understanding Options Pricing

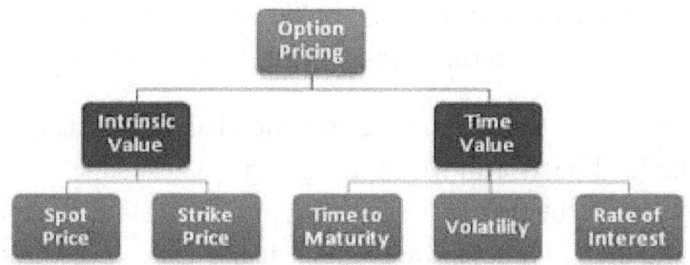

When it comes to trading options successfully, one of the first things you need to do is understand just how it is that options are assigned their relative value. Everything told, the price is made up of a combination of the expected dividends the underlying stock will produce, the interest rates, volatility, time value, intrinsic value and the current stock price. Of these, the volatility, time value, intrinsic value and current stock price play the largest minute to minute role in determining what you are going to pay for the options you purchase.

When it comes to deciding if a potential option is right for you, it is important to understand the difference between any premiums (profits) that the trade might generate and the theoretical value of the option in question. The premium is the amount the buyer is going to pay to get what is specific in the option as well as the money the seller will receive after they have written the option. By contrast, the theoretical value of an option is the amount the option should be worth based on all of the current market signs.

Biggest influences

Current stock price: When it comes to how the current stock price affects any related options, the two move as expected, though there is not a 1 to 1 correlation between them. In general, as prices rise, the price of calls will as increase and the price of puts will decrease and the reverse will occur if the price of the underlying stock is decreasing.

Intrinsic Value: The intrinsic value is the amount of value that the underlying stock is guaranteed to keep, even while the time value continues to decrease over time. To determine the intrinsic value of a call option you can either divide the underlying stocks current price by that price after the strike price of the related call has been subtracted from it. Conversely, you can find the intrinsic value of a put option by subtracting the price of the put from the current stock price and then dividing that result by the current stock price.

The result in either case will be a reflection of the type of advantage that exercising the option in question would generate. Essentially, it can be seen as the minimum amount you will get from the option. For example, if there is a company whose stock is currently selling at roughly $34.80 then a call option of $30 would intrinsically be valued at $4.80 because $34.80-$30=$4.80. If this were a put option, then it would have no intrinsic value because $30-$34.80=-4.80 and a negative intrinsic value is inherently 0.

Time Value: The time value is related to the amount of time an option has left and can more effectively be thought of as the likelihood with which it is going to exceed the amount of its intrinsic value. To determine the time value for any option you simply take the price of the option in question and then subtract the amount of its intrinsic value. As a rule of thumb, expect your options to lose around 30 percent of its value in the first 50 percent of its time on the market with the other 70 percent decreasing over the remainder of its time.

Continuing with the company with shares at $34.80 as discussed above, if the related contract is 30 days away from expiring and the related call option is currently going for $5 then the time value for the call is going to be set at 20 cents because $5 (the cost of the option) is subtracted from $4.80 (the intrinsic value). Alternatively, if the same stock was related to an option that is currently worth $6.85 that was not going to expire for 9 months then it would have a time value of $2.05 because $6.85 subtracted from $4.80 is $2.05. Regardless, the intrinsic value stays the same and the remainder of the price fluctuates based on the resulting time value.

The time value is also directly affect by the amount of volatility the stock in question is likely to experience in the time frame given. If the stock is expected to remain stable, the related time value cost would be low. The opposite is true for stocks with a high rate of volatility because the likelihood that they are going to change drastically before their expiration date is much greater.

Volatility: While it is extremely important to measure correctly, volatility is the most subjective of all of the primary influences which can make it difficult to do so properly, especially for new options traders. Luckily there are several calculators that can be used to help successfully determine volatility. Additionally, there are numerous types of volatility, though historical and implied volatility are the two you should concern yourself with in the moment.

Historical volatility is the amount of volatility the underlying stock in question has seen in the past. It helps to illuminate potential future movements; specifically, how major they are likely going to be. Looking at the historical volatility will make it easier to determine the appropriate exercise price you will want to choose. Implied volatility is the amount of volatility the underlying stock has in the moment based on the current state of the market and relevant related prices. It can be used to help you accurately determine the potential of a possible trade.

Chapter 4: Treating Option Trading as a Business

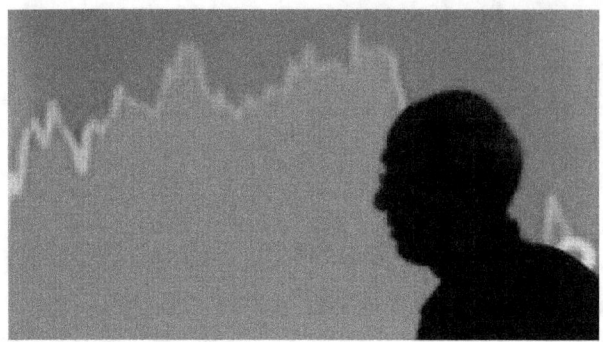

In this chapter we will move on to the management and business skills that you will need to adapt to become a successful Option trader. This is simply because trading options is a business albeit with unique situations but it does require its own management style. No matter what you trade, you are a business manager running a financial trading business. Therefore you must become comfortable understanding the costs associated with operating the business as this help you budget accordingly. In business a simple equation of Profits = Cash Income – Operating Expenses, will dictate how profitable a business is being run. Therefore your goal as a business manager will be to maximize profits and an easy way to do that is control or minimize operating expenses.

Now as a beginner, operating expenses may be high as initially certain costs will be unavoidably higher. This is because you will likely be paying more for a broker platform, education and your trading losses. But that's all part of the learning curve that any beginner must expect when they start trading. However, as you become more experienced and your trading skills and strategies evolve, many of those starter costs will go down. However as you get more experienced you will start to realize the need for more complex strategies and market analysis tools so subscriptions to analysis platforms and data services will likely go up.

Nonetheless, always keep in mind that Option trading for you is a business and that some early losses are part of those operating expenses. The goal of course should be to manage the risk and thereby minimize it but the nature of trading makes it impossible to eliminate risk. Managing risk is very doable and is done by disciplines fund management through determining proper trade allocation amounts and setting maximum loss per trade.

Starting out you should never be risking more than 1%-3% of your fund on any one trade. Options trading is far more flexible than most other types of financial trading in allowing this due of course to the lower prices and the power of leverage. And although effectively executing trades is one way of minimizing losses, designing reliable fund management and a trading plan is the foundation of a successful trading career, which will be judged on longevity.

Controlling your emotions

It one thing being keen and wager to start trading but it's quite another to start to trade without a deep understanding of what you are actually doing. If for example you just jump in with little market knowledge you will be gambling using your limited knowledge. This can lead to emotional trading whereby you can start reacting to price movements in an irrational manner. Humans are after all irrational creatures and we tend to stick with something long after we should have chucked it as a bad deal. This is a form of what is called cognitive bias which leads us to continue to throw good money after bad because we think we must turn around our losses. The problem is that emotional trading is usually the path to even bigger losses. That's why we have to understand the rules about sunk costs – went it's lost it is lost, forget it and move on. When we have strict rules that free us from chasing losses and allow us to let go we can then start to consider each trade as a separate entity with no correlation or connection with anything that has gone before. Then we can start to trade rationally and logically. And this is why you need to design an anticipatory trading plan.

A suitable trading plan should have these basic ingredients:

- That you have the technology that you need to trade efficiently such as a computer, fast internet and mobile devices that will allow you to work anywhere
- Time Management: You need to plan your working hours so that you can commit time to trading. Short term positions will require more of your time so allocate the hours necessary to monitor your trading position
- Good Communication: Build up and have to hand a collection of reliable and trusted real-time quote table and option chain services.
- Reliable Trade Execution: Work with an online broker that has a good reputation for efficiently and accurately executing trades.
- Education: A trading plan must take into account provisions for developing your skills. This should include working on enhancing your technical and fundamental analysis skills. You will also need to develop good option chain and chart reading skills in order to find appropriate options and opportunities.

Chapter 5: Trading Options for Profit

Now the whole purpose of trading is that you want to have more money in the future than what you have just now. Therefore, to increase your wealth you are trading Options supplied by the markets. But here is the thing, regardless of the time frame — the question will come down to whether you have a tendency to hold a position for a short or long time — your objective after all will be the same too make more money.

But here is the problem because that hunger to make a profit makes traders and especially beginners impatient. Therefore as a beginner you should consider that every time that you contemplate a new trading strategy you will also have to contemplate a new learning curve. As a result, be prepared to realize that every change in strategy or trading tactics will begin with a deep study and analysis of trade conditions. This is where paper trading or virtual trading becomes invaluable as it lets you experiment with virtual cash and practice tactics with zero risks. Always be careful that when you start to trade with real cash that losses can be amplified so always be patient and be prepared to diligently spend the time required learning how to trade safely, or you will likely lose a lot of money on worthless premiums.

Regardless of the type of financial trading that you are undertaking there are some simple steps that you should adhere to in order to trade safely. It doesn't matter if you are a beginner or an intermediary trader it is always sensible to ensure that you protect your capital. This means that even if you are experienced in other forms of trading or investing, or even have experience with options but with different assets, you should always seriously contemplate the following:

- Check your financial health

This means simply to check your financial balance sheet and your disposable income. This is hugely important as before you start trading in Options or any other financial instrument you must realize how much you can afford to lose. Therefore you must go over your finances diligently, and make sure that the amount that you have as trading capital is indeed disposable income. This means reviewing your current loans, mortgages, and life and health insurances as well as school fees or college funds.

- Draw up a financial net worth statement

The purpose here is to ensure that you are aware of the amount you could lose and the desire to make profits – be sure you are comfortable with the risk/reward ratio. Also try and make sure that your finances are healthy and understand why you are taking on extraordinary risk.

- Be realistic

Don't chase unrealistic goals and trade beyond your experience or safe capital levels. Furthermore, never risk more than 5% of your capital on any one trade – for beginners 1%-3% is the recommended maximum.

- Know your own risk appetite

If you are a typically a cautious trader or a gambler, that may indicate that you may not be a good options trader. Nonetheless, there may be many trading option tactics and strategies that will suit your risk appetite. The thing to remember is that once you understand the built-in safety nets that trading options provides then it will decrease your risk. An important caveat is that just make sure you read through the book and stick to the beginners' strategies and tactics and find the ones that make you comfortable before you jump in.

- Analyze the Data

Stocks trading places a lot of emphasis on technical analysis, fundamental analysis and Charts in order to maximize your chances of trading options successfully. Option trading rides upon the underlying stock so it also places a high emphasis on improving your technical and fundamental analysis skills. Therefore, you should be a diligent analyst, especially in identifying and following the dominant trends, as well as being able to analyze charts and the behavior of the underlying assets in your options.

- Always test your strategies before putting them into practice

Testing out scenarios and tactics beforehand through paper trading before you take real-life risks is essential. Testing out theories before committing them with real money is always an excellent idea that is certain to provide both practices as well as saving you a lot of money

- Never trade with money that you aren't willing to lose

This might seem strange as Options are often seen as being risk management tools. But even though options are often deemed to be risk-management vehicles, you can still lose money trading them – sometimes in the case of insurance that is the whole purpose. And if you should adopt more sophisticated and riskier option strategies; your potential losses should always be identified and accepted as they could be significant if your trades – especially- sell- if they are not thoroughly investigated and analyzed beforehand.

Chapter 6: Starter Strategies

While it can be easy to feel as though there is too much information out there regarding options trading to ever hope to really keep it straight, there are several key strategies you will use on a regular basis that you can focus on at the start to make the entire process far more manageable. As long as you take the time to utilize them correctly, you will find that each of the strategies outlined below will dramatically improve your success rate while decreasing your overall risk at the same time.

Keep in mind that the strategies that you use aren't nearly as important as the fact that you choose strategies that suit your personal trading style and compliments the trading plan you are focused on using for the time being. Keep in mind that just because a strategy seems useful, doesn't mean it is going to be useful in your hands.

Play name: **Buy/write**

Who should run it: This strategy is suitable for everyone

When to run it: This strategy is effective in a bearish market

Details: Sometimes referred to as the covered call, this strategy works when the trader purchases shares of an underlying stock while at the same time generating a call that is equal to the entire number of underlying stock shares owned. This strategy is ideal for traders who have already invested in the stock market and are looking for a way to shore up what may be previously questionable choices as the options will ensure that you are able to generate a premium even if the other bets placed in the investment don't exactly pay off. This is an especially viable way to ensure long term investments remain viable as the option will guarantee a profitable price for the length of its existence. This makes the covered call strategy ideal for LEAPs, index future and funds whose purchase was facilitated via margin.

Play name: Married put

Who should run it: This strategy is suitable for everyone

When to run it: This strategy is effective in a bullish market

Details: A married put is a great strategy if you have reason to take a bullish attitude towards the price of a given underlying asset while at the same time aiming to shore up any potential losses you might come across. To use this strategy properly, the first thing you will need to do is to purchase any amount of the underlying asset in question while tat the same time purchasing a put that covers the same amount. This will act as the price floor that will help you to prevent serious, unexpected losses in the case of a sudden price drop. While adding more money to a losing proposition is never the best choice, a married put can be used to shore up an existing investment that hasn't turned out as you hoped. Regardless of the size of your portfolio, this is a useful strategy to mitigate risk that can't be dealt with in any other way.

While the married put will not be the best choice in any situation, if used in the right way, and with plenty of caution, it can be a reliable way to improve your successful trading percentage successfully. To ensure this always works out in your favor, you will never want to begin a new transaction without having a clear understanding of the risk you are working with beforehand. You will then be able to factor in additional costs more easily and compare the total cost to the amount of risk you are going mitigate as a result.

After that, all that's left is going to be doing the math and choosing the option that makes the most fiscal sense at the moment. What's more, married puts also help to reduce the potential for risk when it comes to early options to exercise as it ensures you always have available shares waiting in the wings.

Play name: Bull call spread

Who should run it: This strategy is suitable for everyone

When to run it: This strategy is effective in a bullish market

Details: To utilize the bull call spread successfully, you will want to start with a call option that is purchased at a strike price that is worth returning to in the future. You will also need to sell an equal number of calls at a strike price that is above the initial strike price yet still within a reasonable distance. Both of these calls will also need to include the same timeframe as well as the same underlying asset. This is an excellent strategy to use if you feel bullish on the strength of the asset in question or you have research that shows the price is likely to increase during your chosen timeframe.

This strategy also goes by the name vertical credit spread thanks to its mismatched legs. Those that sell close to the money result in a credit spread that includes a positive time value and a net credit. Debit spreads are created if a short option ends further away from the money than the point it started from. Regardless, you can consider this strategy a net buy.

Play name: Bear put spread

Who should run it: This strategy is suitable for everyone

When to run it: This strategy is effective in a bearish market

Details: Similar in practice to the bull call spread, the bear put spread is useful under opposite circumstances. To use it effectively you will need to purchase a pair of put options that have different strike prices, own lower and one higher. You will then need to purchase an equal number with the same timeframe and the same underlying asset. This can be an especially useful strategy if you have a bearish opinion of the underlying asset in question as it will help to limit your losses if you judge the market incorrectly. It is still important to be cautious, however, as the profits that it will bring you are always going to be limited to the difference between the two puts you initially purchased, minus any relevant fees.

The most profitable time to utilize this strategy is if you are already planning on short selling a specific underlying asset and a traditional put option won't provide you with the protection you need. You will likely find them especially useful if you plan on speculating and also feel that prices are going to decrease. This will allow you to avoid employing additional capital while only waiting for the worst to happen. As such, you will be able to hope for the best and plan for the worst at the same time.

Play name: Protective collar

Who should run it: This strategy is suitable for everyone

When to run it: This strategy is effective in a bullish or bearish market

Details: The protective collar strategy can be executed by buying into a put option that is already out of the money. From there, you will then want to write a secondary call option that is based on the same underlying asset and is also out of the money. After that, you will then be able to create a secondary call option that is based on the same underlying asset that is also out of the money already. Thus, this strategy is useful if you are already committed to a long position on an underlying asset that has a history of strong gains. Using a protective collar properly then allows you to ensure that you can anticipate a steady level of profit while also retaining control of the underlying asset if the positive trend does continue.

Using a protective collar correctly is as easy as ensuring the contract for the put option you purchased was at a strike price that is more than likely enough to ensure you will hold onto most of the profits you banked throughout the process. After that, you will then be able to fund the collar strategy using the call option you previously created. This strategy is extremely useful if you are looking to maintain your profits at all costs as it only requires a small additional fee. What's more, this is an excellent way to move funds about got tax purposes as any option that you roll over does not need to be accounted for until it has been either purchased or expired.

Play name: **Straddle**

Who should run it: This strategy is suitable for everyone

When to run it: This strategy is effective in a bullish or bearish market

Details: The straddle can be used to either go long or short. The long straddle can be extremely effective if you feel as though the price of a given underlying asset is going to move significantly in one direction, you just don't know what direction that will ultimately be. To utilize this strategy, you will need to purchase a put and a call, both using the same underlying asset, strike price and timeframe. After the long straddle has been created successfully you will be guaranteed to generate a profit if the price in question moves in either direction before it expires.

On the other hand, if you are interested in utilizing a short straddle, you will instead want to sell a call and a put with the same costs, timeframe and underlying asset. This will allow you to profit from the premium, even if everything else doesn't turn out as well as you may have liked. This guaranteed profit means that this is a particularly useful strategy if you don't expect to see movement very much in either direction before the option expires. Nevertheless, it is still important to remember that the chances that this strategy will be successful are directly related to the odds that the underlying asset is going to move in the first place.

Play name: **Strangle**

Who should run it: This strategy is suitable for everyone

When to run it: This strategy is effective in a bullish or bearish market

Details: Functionally, a strangle is similar to a straddle except that it is often cheaper to execute on as you are buying into options that are already out of the money. As such, you can typically pay as much as 5o percent the cost of a straddle for a strangle which makes it even easier to play both sides of the fence. Typically, a long strangle is more useful than a short straddle because it offers up twice the premium for the same amount of risk.

To use the long strangle correctly, you will want to purchase a call along with a put that are both based on the same underlying asset with the same timeframe and different strike prices. The strike price for the call will need to be above the strike price for the put and both should be out of the money. This strategy can be especially useful if you plan on the underlying asset moving a great deal, without having a clear idea as to the direction. When used properly, this will virtually ensure you turn a profit once you have taken any fees out of the equation.

Play name: Butterfly spread

Who should run it: This strategy is suitable for everyone

When to run it: This strategy is effective in a neutral market

Details: A butterfly spread is a combination of a bear spread and a traditional bull strategy which uses a total of three strike points. To begin with, you will need to purchase a call option at the lowest point you can manage before selling a pair of calls at a higher price and then a third call that has an ever-higher price. Your end goal with these purchases is to make sure that you have a range of prices you can profit from when everything is said and done.

This strategy can prove particularly effective when you have a completely neutral opinion on the current market. What's more, you should also expect the underlying asset to move in the direction you favor, even if you don't have all the details locked down just yet. This, then means that you will want to strive to keep the market volatility as low as possible. In fact, the greater the overall level of volatility, the greater the cost of this strategy will be. Furthermore, it is extremely important to keep in mind that if you choose incorrectly when it comes to the direction the underlying asset is going to move, then the amount you stand to lose can be significant.

Play name: Iron condor

Who should run it: This strategy is suitable for everyone

When to run it: This strategy is effective in a bullish or bearish market

Details: To utilize the iron condor strategy, you will need to begin by taking a short position as well as a long position via a pair of strangles that are situated so they will take full advantage of a market that is staunchly low volatility. The pair of strangles should include both a long and a short, with both set to the outer strike price. You can accomplish the same general effect with a pair of credit spreads if you are so inclined. In this scenario, the call spread would be placed above the market price and the put would be placed beneath the current market price.

The iron condor should only be used if you are trading via index options as they offer the decreased level of volatility and risk that you need in order to make it reliable. This means that you will want to use the iron condor if you are practically certain the market is going to move in the direct your research indicates that it is going to. Doing otherwise is almost surely going to leave your plan open to significant additional risk, and likely sooner rather than later as well.

Play name: Iron Butterfly

Who should run it: This strategy is suitable for everyone

When to run it: This strategy is effective in a bullish or bearish market

Details: The iron butterfly strategy can be anchored by either a short straddle or a long straddle depending on your needs. Regardless, you will want to then orchestrate a strangle based on the straddle you needed to use. The iron butterfly utilizes a mixture of puts and calls to limit the potential for loss (but also profits) around the strike price you previously determined. This strategy is best used with options that are out of the money as they allow you to minimize both risk and cost.

Chapter 7: Strategies for Making the Best of a Bad Situation

When it comes to trading options successfully in the long-term, the secret isn't being able to make the right trades at every juncture. After all, that's impossible. No, the true secret to long-term success is learning to recover when a surefire trade suddenly goes sideways on you at the last moment. The faster you can get your trade back on track, the faster you can get back to making a profit.

Long call repair strategies

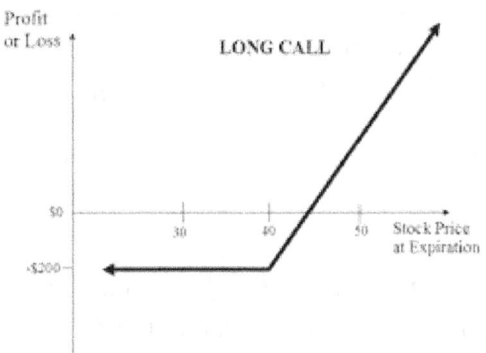

This first section contains strategies designed to increase the profit potential of long call positions that have recently seen a quick, unrealized loss. Remember, having a great strategy is extremely important, but there is more to making a profit in the long-term than that. In trading, the best offense is often a good defense.

Play name: Long call repair

Who should run it: This strategy is suitable for veterans

When to run it: This strategy is effective in a bullish market

Details: It is common for new traders to buy a simple put or call, only to find out that they were ultimately wrong about the way the underlying asset moved when everything was said and done. For example, a long call that is out of the money would see sudden unrealized losses if its underlying asset dropped. To understand the best course of action in this situation, a secondary example is required. For this example, assume that it is the middle of the February and you believe that Microsoft which is currently sitting at 93.30 is about to make a move that puts it above its resistance levels and end at about 95. You can then easily jump in with a near the money call for July, leaving you roughly six months until expiration and plenty of time for the related movement to occur.

From there, however, things don't go according to plan and the stock drops to below $90 instead. The price of your July call would now be worth only about $1.25, down from about $3 thanks to the time decay, creating an unrealized loss of $175 per option purchased. As there is still a fair amount of time left until expiration, it is possible that the stock could still make the option profitable but waiting also has the potential to generate additional losses or other opportunity costs which could also result in a loss of profit.

One way to mitigate this loss is through the process of averaging down and purchasing additional options, though this only increases your risk if things continue to not go your way. Instead, a simple and effective means of lowering your breakeven point, while also increasing the possibility of turning a profit is to roll the position down into a bull call spread, discussed in the next chapter. The concept of rolling it down simply means to replace an existing option with a new option that is similar in most ways except that one has a lower strike price than the other. Utilizing this practice mans you don't have to exercise the initial option as the time is extended until the end of the second option.

To use this strategy in the above example, you would start by placing an order to sell a pair of calls at the July expiration date at your target price of $95 for $1.25, which is essentially going short on the initial call option. At the same time, you would want to buy an additional July 90 call and sell it for roughly $2.90. The result of this process is a bull call spread that improves the odds of success while only adding a small amount of addition risk. What' smore, the breakeven point decreases dramatically from $98, all the way to $93.25.

From there, assuming that the Microsoft stock continued to trade even higher, past the original starting point, then your bull call spread would be strong enough to break even with a potential profit for the target of $95, though the maximum amount of profit for each option is going to be $175 due to the way it was constructed.

Play name: Alternate repair style

Who should run it: This strategy is suitable for veterans

When to run it: This strategy is effective in a bullish market

Details: Alternately, you could roll down into a traditional butterfly spread, discussed in the next chapter, when the underlying stock drops to $90. When using this strategy, you would instead want to sell a pair of July $90 calls, which would sell for about $4 each, while also hanging on to the July $95 long call. You would also need to purchase a call for the July date at $85 as well that sells for around $7.30 after time decay has been taken into account.

You will see that the total risk actually decreases on the downside in this scenario as the total debit amount drops to $230, and there is also a limited upside risk if the stock moves back towards the breakeven point. If the stock goes nowhere, the trade actually still turns a profit as well.

Play name: Combined repair strategy

Who should run it: This strategy is suitable for all-starts

When to run it: This strategy is effective in a bullish market

Details: As this is a variation of the traditional butterfly spread, the maximum amount of profit you can expect is going to come at the strike price of the two July $90 short calls that you created, but movement dropping away from this point until it starts to generate losses instead. As such, you may also wan tot combine the two repair strategies to create a multi-lot repair approach. This combination can be used to preserve the ideal odds that come with producing a profit from a potential loss.

Determining strike price: One of the most important facets of using the repair strategy effectively is setting the correct strike price for the options in question. This price will ultimately determine the cost of the trade as well as influencing your breakeven point. The best place to start is by considering the magnitude of the unrealized loss that you are coming off of. For example, if you purchased a stock at $40 and it is now at $30 then your paper loss is $10 per share.

In this case, you would want to purchase the at the money calls while at the same time writing out of the money calls with a higher strike price that is above the strike price of the purchased calls by half of the stock's loss. This means you would want to start with three-month options before moving forward from there as needed. Generally speaking, the greater the loss you have already experienced, the greater the amount of time that you will have to spend repairing it.

It is also important to keep in mind that it will not be possible to repair all mistakes for free as the worst offenders will require a small debit payment in order to set up the position in a potentially profitable manner. If your loss is over 70 percent, then it is likely not going to be possible to repair it at all.

Unwind the position: While breaking even after the hypothetical situations discussed above might sound good now, when you find yourself in a similar situation in the real world you may find yourself wanting to more than just break even, you will likely want to make an additional profit as well. As an example, assume that the Microsoft stock that previously dropped now rose to $60, which means that you are now interested in keeping it rather than selling when it hits $70.

Unwinding a position consists of closing out a positive that has previously been pulling double duty offsetting alternate investments. Unwinding can increase liquidity risk in some scenarios. If an asset is less liquid it can be difficult to find an interested buyer or seller which means the liquidity risk is elevated. Regardless of whether a transaction was completed intentionally or accidentally, all risks associated with the particular security still apply when attempting to unwind it.

Unwinding becomes an even more advantageous proposition if the volatility in the underlying stock has increased to such a point that you decide you want to hold onto the stock. You will be able to find your options priced much more attractively in this scenario as long as you remain in a good position with the underlying stock.

Problems can arise in this scenario if you make an attempt at exiting while the stock is trading at or above the break-even price as this will cost you as the total value of the option in question will be negative. As such, you should generally only consider unwinding an existing position if the price remains underneath the original break-even price and the future prospects look promising. Otherwise, you are typically going to be better off simply establishing a new position in the same stock at the current market price.

Short call repair strategies

Play name: Delta hedge

Who should run it: This strategy is suitable for veterans

When to run it: This strategy is effective in a bullish or bearish market

Details: To understand this strategy, consider the following. Let's say you own an exchange traded call option on a listed stock (very general case). If available in sufficient quantity, borrow and sell the underlying security that the call option was written on (short sell it). You'll be long the call and short the stock. This is called a delta hedge, as you would be delta trading the stock. Delta refers to short-term price volatility.

In other words, you'll short a single large block of the stock, then buy shares, in small increments, whenever the market drops slightly, on an intra-day basis. When the market price of the stock rises incrementally, you'll sell a few shares. Back and forth, in response to short-term market price moves, while maintaining a static "hedge ratio". As your original call option gets closer to maturity, roll it over into the next available contract, either one-month, or preferably three-month, time to expiration.

Play name: Synthetic Short

Who should run it: This strategy is suitable for veterans

When to run it: This strategy is effective in a bearish market

Details: The synthetic short is used to promote the payoff of a losing short position. It can be completed by selling a call that is currently at the money while at the same time buying an equal number of puts that are also at the money for the same underlying stock and expiration date. It is important to keep in mind that there are unlimited risks when it comes to using this strategy, along with an unlimited potential for profit which means it is best used when you are bearish on the related underlying security.

You can think of this strategy as being similar to the short stock position as a whole as there is no maximum for profit as long as the underlying stock price continues to drop. Furthermore, a credit is typically taken when entering this scenario as calls are almost always going to be more expensive than puts. This means that even if the underlying stock price remains relatively unchanged for the length of the expiration time there will still be a potential for profit based on the amount of the initial credit that was taken. The formula for determining a profit in this scenario is as follows:

Maximum Profit = Unlimited

Profit Achieved When Price of Underlying < Strike Price of Long Put + Net Premium Received

Profit = Strike Price of Long Put - Price of Underlying + Net Premium Received

As with the unlimited potential for reward, the potential for risk in this scenario, to determine the potential for loss, consider the following:

Maximum Loss = Unlimited

Loss Occurs When Price of Underlying > Strike Price of Short Call + Net Premium Received

Loss = Price of Underlying - Strike Price of Short Call - Net Premium Received + Commissions Paid

Finally, the breakeven point in this scenario can be determined via the following:

Breakeven Point = Strike Price of Long Put + Net Premium Received

Chapter 8: The concept of moneyness

The Scale of "Moneyness"

Low Level of Moneyness   High Level of Moneyness

| Commodities & | Securities & various | Foreign currencies | Govt money or | Bank deposits or |
| other goods | claims on money | SDRs & Gold | "outside money" | "inside money" |

The term moneyness is used in Options trading to describe the financial status of an Option. An option is said to be **in the money**— or profitable to exercise if its strike price is lower than the price of the underlying asset. For example it would be in the money if you could exercise your rights to buy the underlying stock at the strike price to immediately sell on the market for a profit.

However, the concept of moneyness has a few different aspects to it.

Remember that the strike price is the locked-in price that the underlying stock can be bought or sold for, if exercised. Therefore the strike price is an important factor in determining the Options value as we can compare the Options strike price with the actual market price of the stock. This relationship between the strike and actual market price determines the intrinsic value of the Option and will be a determining factor:

- At the money: This is when the strike price and the stock price is the same and so it applies to both calls and puts
- Near the money: As it is unlikely for the strike and actual price to exactly match any close to equality is termed near the money
- In the money: This is when the strike price in a call option is below the price of the actual stock. On the other hand with a put option the strike price is in the money when it is above the stock price
- Out of the money: This is when a call option strike price is above the stock price. With a put option the strike price will be out of the money when it is below the stock price

As you start to practice and gain experience working with quote tables and orders, you will become very familiar with these terms. This is because you will soon become accustomed to using the relationship between the stock price and the strike price to determine if there is any intrinsic value in the Option. A thing to remember is that only options that are "in the money" will have any intrinsic value.

Indeed, an option will be said to be **in the money** only if it is profitable to exercise. It is **out of the money** if it is not profitable. This means that just because the strike price is above or below the actual price doesn't automatically make it in the money as we must always consider the cost of the premium. Also, the relationship of the underlying price to the strike price depends on the type of option involved.

In other words, a long call is in the money if the strike price is less than the underlying stock price. Therefore you would make a profit if you to exercise your rights under the option, by buying the underlying asset, and then selling it at the higher market price. On the other hand, if the underlying stock price is less than the strike price, then the option is out of the money.

Conversely for the writer of the option, the trader that is obliged to fulfil the holder's rights whether that is to buy or to sell, then they will have the opposite point of view. For the writer of the Option has taken a short position and will be out of the money when the price of the underlying asset is greater than the strike price and in the money when the price of the underlying asset is less than the exercise.

Similarly, the positions are reversed when we consider relative perspectives of the holder and writer of the put option. For example, if the holder of a put option has a strike price of $35 and if the underlying stock is trading at more than $35, then they would be out of the money as it would not be profitable to exercise, so the long put position would be out of the money. However the holders long put would be in the money if the underlying were to trade at less than $35.

But conversely, if we consider the short put position, we will find that an underlying price of more than $35 would mean the option would not be exercised by the holder, so the writer could keep the premium and be in the money. But, if the underlying stock price were to fall below $35, then the option would be in the money from the holder's perspective as it could be exercised at a profit and the writer's short position would now be out of the money.

The following table offers a neat summary of it all.

The Moneyness of an Option

Position	In the Money	Out of the Money
Long call	Stock > Strike	Stock < Strike
Short call	Stock < Strike	Stock > Strike
Long put	Stock < Strike	Stock > Strike

| Short put | Stock > Strike | Stock < Strike |

Stock = current market price of the underlying stock (variable)

Strike = the locked-in strike price of the Option (fixed)

As we can see the holder and the writer of the Options always have an opposite position except when the strike price and the underlying price are the same, then the option is **at the money or near the money.** This is regardless of the type of option whether it is a put or a call, or whether you are going long or short.

Furthermore, the moneyness of an option is not affected by the style of the option. What this means is that even with a European option, which can only be exercised at the expiry time, it can still transition many times during that period often jumping between being in, out, or at the money at any given time.

Open Interest

An interesting metric that is often included in quote tables for Option contracts is an indicator depicting Open interest, which is the total number of outstanding options contracts. Open interest is tallied at the end of each day. Open interest is used as a metric for the measurement of market sentiment. It should not be misinterpreted as the number of options traded because it is not the same thing as volume as many options are traded to close out existing positions.

However if you are speculating in short term trading of options then Open Interest is an important metric as you will want as much market interest as you can get on your option. This will make it easier to trade when you choose to exit the position as there will likely be many potential buyers.

Expiration and Exercise

Options expire at regular intervals determined by the expiration date, which is the date the option expires. Most options expire on the third Friday of a given month. However, some high-volume weekly options have expiration dates every Friday. The last time to trade the option is at the close of the market immediately before the option expires. Some European options close earlier (sometimes on a Thursday but the closing time would be specified for the option, and most broker apps track the options expiry dates and send a notification so you'd know):

The option period is the term used to denote the valid time **until** expiration and it starts the moment the option is made (written) and ends on the expiry day. However, there are ways to stay in the position if you want to beyond the expiry date. If you want to maintain the position you can **roll** by closing your current – soon to expire - open position and simultaneously make a new position at a different strike price or expiration.

Exercising your Rights

To **exercise** is the term used to cash in an option but the vast majority of options are never exercised. But should you want to and you have a call option giving you the right to buy shares of ABC at $100 per share, and the stock is trading at $105, all you have to do is notify your broker that you want to exercise the Option.

When exercising your option to buy the stock you will need to have the funds in your account. Almost all brokers will require that you buy – pay for the stock – before you sell. This means that you will need sufficient funds in your account before you can exercise your position. Some brokers allow you to turn around and sell the stock immediately and you may get away with selling the stock before you pay the broker, but that type of free-riding - is frowned up.

Delivery and Settlement

When a call option on a stock is exercised, the writer has to transfer the shares to the option buyer's account at the strike price. If the writer is not covered by already owning the stock they must go and buy the shares in the open market.

However, if there is an option for **cash settlement,** then the person whose option is profitable receives a cash transfer payment. This is more commonly used in trading in index options.

Extrinsic and Intrinsic Value

Options have two primary sources of value. The **intrinsic value** is the option's strike price in relation to the price of the underlying asset. An option has intrinsic value only if it is in the money. If it is not in the money then there is no profit so no value.

Time value, on the other hand is known as **extrinsic value.** This value is the difference between the option's price and the amount of intrinsic value - the amount it is in the money. The logic behind this is that the amount that an option is in the money is its intrinsic value, the profit should you claim it today.

But the option can be worth more today than the profit you would realize if you exercised it. This is an important consideration when you are hedging as you do not want to exercise the option – take the profit. Instead you value the time remaining on the insurance value of the option. This additional time value cannot be ignored as it explains why people will often hold onto options when they are profitable to exercise. Of course they may just be riding a trend and hoping to end up with a larger profit.

Nonetheless, it is important to realize that Options do have both extrinsic value and intrinsic value. The more you understand the components of an option's price, the better you can value the option relative to your needs.

One additional concept of Option value that we must know about is **parity**. When we refer to Parity with regards to an Options value we mean the point where an option is in the money but has no time value. Options generally don't reach parity until just before expiration.

Weighing Option Costs and Benefits

There are many advantages to trading using options, but you don't get all those benefits without taking on-board some element of risk. A notable risk that you have to accept is that options have a limited lifespan as they are limited by an expiry date. Now there are clear strategies that you must have in place when handling this risk such as having an exit strategy. For example your choices are, trade the option during the timespan of the option, expire the option on or before the expiry date or simply let the option expire.

However, there can be a big problem with just leaving options to expire. For example, if the option is in-the-money at expiration, your broker may well automatically exercise/assign the option. The problem here is that by exercising the valuable option they have effectively converted a low-cost option position into a high-cost stock position, which you may not want or be able to afford. Consequently, you need to carefully monitor your options and check for notifications from the broker platform regarding any in-the-money option positions, which are nearing the expiration date. You need to do this in anticipation of this likely change in your margin requirement. Alternatively you want to make sure you have sufficient time to trade the option or make other adjustments such as rolling over a trade in order to avoid buying the stock.

Risk of Leverage

Another significant risk to be aware of is that of leverage. Because Options don't cost much as stock as they are simply a contract, this means that they experience disproportionately larger percentage price gains in reaction to the far more expensive underlying stock's very small price movements. The huge benefit of this is that it results in large percentage gains when the underlying stock moves in the anticipated direction by even a small amount. The downside though is that it also results in a 100% wipe-out of the investment if the stock moves by even the smallest amount in the wrong direction. This is not necessarily an issue with beginners or at least it shouldn't be as the risk manifests itself mainly through trading too large a position size. However, you need to be aware that as beneficial as leverage clearly is, it can also be a double edge sword, so be aware that leverage is a risk that needs to be addressed. One simple way to nullify or minimize this level of risk is to keep your position size small.

Lastly, Options as we know possess a time value (extrinsic value) in addition to their inherent intrinsic value (in the money value), which is also another double-edged sword. For option buyers, time-decay acts as a headwind because it is continually decreasing the value of the option. By doing so this increases the dependency on greater stock price movement to break even on the trade. For option writers, it acts as a tailwind because it allows a profit to be generated through steady premium incomes regardless of whether the stock moves or not.

Two other option cost factors should be considered:

1. Costs associated with the trading process
2. Cost of exercising the stock

By understanding the basic cost structure for an option, you can see how options also add through leverage an element of risk, despite the fact that options also provide leverage at a reduced risk.

To complicate the matter a little is the fact that Option prices are partially based on probabilities. For stock options, you want to consider the likelihood that a particular option will be in-the-money before or at expiration given the type of price movements the underlying stock has recently undergone. The way an Option is valued takes into consideration 6 factors; Stock price, strike price, time to expiration, interest rates and dividends but there is a wildcard factor – volatility.

Trading rules you should know

Whenever you begin trading a new market, you'll need to become acquainted very quickly with the trading rules. Usually your broker or their trading platform will prevent you from going wrong but you shouldn't need to rely on them to keep you right. In this section we provide a short list of common basic rules for trading Options that will hopefully help you through your initial trading executions and throughout your trading career:

- Contract pricing: In general Options trade in increments of $0.01, $0.05, and $0.10.
- Option premium: The price of the premium that you pay for an option is obtained by multiplying the option price offered by the multiplier. When trading in stocks the multiplier value is usually based upon 100 shares of the underlying stock. Therefore, when you purchase one option that is quoted at $2.80, you are actually going to have to pay $2,80 x 100 = $280 for the option, plus any broker commission.
- Market conditions: There are different market conditions that impact both the stock and options markets. These include the following:
- Trading halts for a security or entire market: If you find yourself holding an option for a halted stock, them the any options based on the stock will also be halted. This does not affect your rights or prevent you from exercising your contract rights. However be aware that when this occurs before expiration it may be difficult to trade the options but will not prevent you from exercising the option on or before the expiry date.
- Fast trading conditions: In fast-moving markets stock prices can change rapidly and you are likely to see quotes changing quickly. As a result when you are placing an order you might find that there are significant delays. This can simply be because your bid is not falling out with the bid-ask spread so is being ignored. Therefore you need to check and if necessary to edit your order to make it more acceptable. Also in fast moving market conditions make sure to use limit orders that are price focused rather than market orders as you may end up paying more than you wanted.
- Booked order: In the case of a booked order – one that a market maker places that improve the current market quote. You may encounter problems filling these types of orders for Options greater than 1 contract and you are likely to only get a partial fill of the order. Be aware of this if using ALL or No parameters on your order.
- Best-execution: Execution quality is a measure of a broker's ability to fill orders at, or better than, the current market for the security. Options exchanges are required to monitor and send a daily exception report to your broker whenever a trade is executed at a price other than at the NBBO, referred to as traded-through. If you are unhappy with the price on transactions or are finding it hard to make a trade on what appears to be competitive prices you will need to contact your Broker for an explanation.

Chapter 9: Risk and Option Parameters

When it comes to options trading, the various types of risk that come into play are referred to as one of the **Greeks.** Each variable is then given a different name and there are different ways to go about ensuring that each has as little of an effect on your trades as possible. Trading without first taking the time to clearly understand each of the Greeks and what they mean would be like driving in a foreign country where you were unfamiliar with the basic rules of the road or even the language the signs are written in.

When you look at placing a put or call on a specific underlying stock, or building your general options trading strategy, it is important to always consider the rewards and risks from three primary areas. The amount of price change, the amount of volatility change and the relevant amount of time value the option has left. For holders of calls, this risk can further be identified as either prices moving in the wrong direction, a decrease in volatility or there not being enough useful time left on the option in question. On the contrary, sellers face the risk of prices moving in the wrong direction and an increase in volatility but never when it comes to the time value.

When options are combined or traded, you will then want to determine the Greeks related to new result, often referred to as the **net Greeks.** This will allow you to determine the new difference between risk and reward and act appropriately. Understanding the various Greeks and what them mean will also allow you to tailor your strategy based on your own aversion to risk. Consider them as starter guideposts to ensure you are on the right track when it comes to seeking out the right options for you. There are numerous Greeks to consider and each are outlined in detail below:

Delta

When it comes to individual options, Delta can be seen as the amount of risk that currently exists that the price of the underlying stock is going to move. If the strike price of an option is the same as the current price of the underlying stock, then that stock can be said to have a Delta of .5. This can further be interpreted as meaning that if the underlying stock moves 1 point, the price of the option will shift .5 points assuming everything else remains the same. The total range Delta can possibly be anywhere from -1 to 1. Puts can be anywhere from -1 to 0 and calls can be anywhere from 0 to 1.

Delta is likely the first measurement of risk that you will always want to consider when it comes to choosing the options that are right for you. It is especially helpful when you are deciding when to buy a put option as you want it to be far enough from the current price to make a profit but not so far as to be unreasonable. In this instance, it is beneficial to know the expected results of paying less in exchange for knowing the Delta is going to be lower as well. This difference can be seen by simply looking at the strike price and watching how it changes in relation to the put price.

As a general rule, the less an option costs, the smaller its Delta is going to be. Delta is often linked to the odds that the option will be worth a profit by the time it expires. For example, if you are looking at an option with a Delta of .52, then you can generally assume, all other things being equal, that the option is slightly more likely than 50 percent to end favorably.

Vega

When a position is taken, the risk of change that comes from the volatility of the underlying stock is referred to as the Vega. The level of volatility that an underlying stock has can change even if the price of the stock in question doesn't change; and regardless of the amount it changes, can affect the possibility of profits significantly. Successful strategies can be built around both low volatility and high volatility as well as neutral volatility in some cases. **Long volatility** options are those that increase in value as their amount of volatility goes up and **short volatility** is when value increases as volatility decreases. Strategies or trades that utilize long volatility are said to have a positive Vega and those that use short volatility are said to have a negative Vega. Options that have a neutral level of volatility can be said to have a neutral Vega as well.

As a general rule, the more time standing between an option and its expiration date, the higher that option's Vega is going to be. This is because time value is proportional to volatility as the longer the timeline, the greater the chance of volatility eventually happening will be. For example, if a certain $4 option's underlying stock is current trading around $90 with a Vega of .1 and a volatility of 20 percent. If the volatility increases just 1 percent that would be seen by an increase of 10 cents to a total of $4.10. If the volatility had instead decreased, the price of the $4 option would have decreased by 10 cents instead, leaving a total of $3.90. The amount of change that is seen in an option with a shorter period is often going to result in larger changes because there is ultimately less time the option will restabilize.

Theta

Theta measure the rate at which the time the option has left is disappearing or decaying. This number is frequently going to be negative for your purposes. The moment you purchase an option, your Theta on that option begins decreasing which means the total value of the option begins to decrease as well because options are considered more valuable the longer the period of time they insure against new risk. If the amount of Delta on an option exceeds the Theta, then the option is considered profitable for the holder. If Theta instead exceeds the Delta, the profits go to the writer.

For example, if an option has a Thea of 0.015 then it is going to be worth 1.5 cents less tomorrow than it is right now. Puts have negative thetas and calls have positive thetas. This is because puts are worth the least when they are about to expire and calls are worth the most because the difference between the starting and ending amounts is going to be at its highest. Additionally, Theta fluctuates day to day as it starts off slow and then builds in intensity the closer the option gets to its ultimate expiration. This explains why long term options attract buyers and short term options are preferred by sellers.

If you are planning a trade that has the market remaining neutral then it is important to take Theta into account, but otherwise it is less likely to play into your strategy. Regardless, a general rule of thumb is to aim to purchase an option with the lowest Theta rate as possible.

Gamma

If Delta can be thought of as the amount of change that the option will experience when the underlying stock changes, then Gamma can be thought of as the measurement of how the Delta is likely going to change over time. Gamma increases as options near the point where the price of the option and the price of the underlying stock intersect and decreases the further below the strike price the price of the underlying stock drops. Larger Gammas are risky, but they also offer higher returns on average. Gamma is also likely to increase as a specific option nears its ultimate expiration date. This can be taken a step further with the Gamma of the Gamma which considers the rate the rate the Delta changes at.

For example, if a stock is trading at about $50 and a related option is currently going for $2. If it has a delta of .4 as well as a gamma of .1, then, if the stock increase by $1 then the delta will see an increase of 10 percent which is also the gamma amount. If volatility is low, then gamma is high when the option in question is above its strike price and low when it is below it. Gamma tends to stabilize when volatility is high and decrease when it is low.

Rho

Rho is the name for the risk relating to if the interest rates related to the option in question are going to change before its expiration. When it comes to choosing the system that is right for you Rho will be unlikely to factor into the equation in most instances. As interest rates increase, call prices will do the same while the price of puts will decrease and the reverse is true when interest rates decrease. Rho values are typically at their peak when the price of the underlying stock cross the price of the option in question. Likewise, this value is always going to be negative when it comes to puts and positive when it comes to calls. Rho values are more important when it comes to long options and virtually irrelevant for most short options.

Find the Greeks

When it comes to determining Greeks, it is important to keep in mind that most strategies will have either a negative or a positive value. For example, a positive Vega position will see gains when volatility rises and a negative Delta position will see a decrease when the underlying stock decreases. Keeping an eye on the Greeks and noting how they change is a key to options trading success in both the short and the long term.

When it comes to finding the Greeks for any option, the first thing you will want to keep in mind is that the results you get are always going to be theoretical, no matter how good they end up looking. They are simply projections based on a mathematical formula with various variables plugged in when needed. These include the bid you are putting on the option, the asking price, the last price, the volume and occasionally the interest.

Chapter 10: Tips for Success

Stay away from calls that are Out of the Money: If a call is not at least at the money then it is not worth your time. While you have likely heard the old adage, buy low and sell high, that is never the right choice in this case as calls that are out of the money are much less likely to get back to where they need to be if you hope to turn a profit on them. This, in turn, amounts to little more than gambling because there are always going to be relatively few indicators that you can rely on to determine if the price is going to stabilize in the time allotted.

It is important to keep in mind that buying an option means knowing what direction an underlying stock is going to move in, but it is just as important to know when it is going to move in that direction. If you misjudge either, then you are likely to lose out on the commission in addition to not being able to use that money in other more profitable ways until the option expires. Don't forget, in order to make money you need the option to increase all the way from out of the money to the strike price if you want to make a profit.

Work out multiple strategies: Eventually you will start to feel constrained by the system or plan that you are utilizing and want to expand into a wider variety of options. When this happens it is important that you work out new plans and strategies instead of trying to force your existing strategy to work in ways that it was not designed to. Certain strategies are always only going to work in certain scenarios and trying to force them to do otherwise is just asking for trouble. What's worse, these faulty decisions are going to taint your overall trade average, making your plan seem worse than it actually is.

Utilize a spread: A long spread is comprised of a pair of options, one with a higher cost and the other with a lower cost. The higher cost option is the one that you will buy and the other is the one that you will sell. Everything about the pair of options should be the same except for their strike prices. When using a spread, it is important that you always keep the time value in mind less you find yourself in a scenario where it serves to limit your profits.

Always be clear on when you will be entering or exiting: Ensuring that you know exactly when you want to start a trade or to exit an existing trade can become more difficult the more your emotions begin to come into play. While it will be difficult to leave money on the table at first, having limits to your trade will keep you from losing much more money than it will ultimately cost you. What's more, when you think about the amount of money that you are likely to gain in the short period between when you should exit a trade and when you ultimately do, the amount saved is typically going to be negligible.

Don't double up: If a trade that appears as though it is going to turn a profit suddenly and unexpectedly moves in the wrong direction, the reaction of many novice options traders is going to be let emotion get the better of you and possibly double down on what is rapidly becoming a bad investment in hopes of making back all of the money that was previously lost. If you find yourself in a situation where you are thinking about doubling down on something questionable you can keep yourself from making the wrong decision by first asking yourself if you would have made the decision if things had gone your way from the start. In nearly all scenarios, cutting your losses and moving forward with a clear head is the preferable action. Remember, there are always more profitable trades on the horizon.

Keep earnings dates in mind: When it comes to maximizing your earnings potential it is important to have a clear idea of when any of the underlying stocks related to your options are going to have to disclose their earnings for the past quarter. Regardless of what the outcome of these calls is going to be, they are sure to generate a fair amount of movement when it comes to the stock in question which means being caught unaware can leave you trading based on information that is suddenly extremely outdated. Option prices typically tend to spike around earnings time as a result.

Additionally, it is important to keep in mind when any underlying stock is going to be paying dividends as well. This is extremely important because unless you exercise the options related to the stocks that are going to be paying dividends then you won't make any money in the process. These dividends can sometimes be assigned earlier than expected which is why you always want to have a firm grasp on the newest information available regarding the dates in question.

Understand the risk of early assignment: It is common for new traders to sell options or months without realizing they are putting themselves at risk until they are handed their first early assignment and are forced to deal with it in any way possible. Early assignment occurs when a holder exercises their rights well before the expiration date of the option in question that you are the writer on and it means you have to fulfill your obligation even if the terms aren't as much in your favor as you would like. If this happens to you the best thing you can do is not to let your emotions get the better of you and instead look for ways to make the best of a bad situation before committing to anything specific.

Commit to spreads only when appropriate: When you are first starting out it can be easy to start a spread, consider all available options and then setting up the remainder of the spread. If you typically find yourself buying a call, finding the best possible moment, and then setting up a sell call then you will likely find yourself in a situation where a sudden change of fortune between the two makes seeing even a marginal return on your investment more difficult than you previously intended. This can easily be presented by committing to a spread all at once as this will provide fewer chances for various variables to sneak in and ruin your calculations.

Trade what you can afford to lose: One of the most difficult lessons for many new options traders to learn is that you must never put more into a trade than you can realistically afford to lose, regardless of how good of a deal the trade appears to be at the time. There is never, ever going to be a trade that is a sure thing which means that luck will always play a factor no matter how air tight your system may have appeared to be in the past. If you typically take bigger risks than you can realistically afford, it isn't a question of if you will learn your lesson, it is a matter of when.

Conclusion

Thank you for making it through to the end of this book, let's hope it was informative and able to provide you with all of the tools you need to achieve your goals whatever they may be.

Options trading is a great way to enter the market with a small amount of capital. The premiums keep changing and you can make a lot of money if you trade wisely and do not take unnecessary risks.

This book has explained all the important facts about the options trade. It has tried to throw light on all the aspects of options trading so that you understand the functioning of the market. Trading is just a psychological game. Both parties are trying to guess the direction of the wind. The seller is taking a bigger risk but the profit of the seller is also sturdy as the seller is an experienced player. You have to understand the psyche of the seller.

Knowledge is power when it comes to trading. It is not a guessing game. You are speculating about the rates and the way the market will behave, yet you must have a plan and reasoning behind the actions. Once in the trade, this knowledge will help you in figuring the market will move and the kind of profits you can expect to make.

The Greeks explained in the last few chapters are of great significance and they help you in understanding your risks. The biggest mistake new traders make is not calculating the real value hidden in the trade. A contract that may look attractive might not have any real value at all. You must pay special attention to that part.

The aim of this book is to explain the main concepts of options trading and how it works. You will have to form strategies to move into the market and you will definitely make a profit.